To Jeffrey Cecil
with friendship
and appreciation!

[signature]

Nature's Sorrows and Nature's Joys

Nature's Sorrows and Nature's Joys

Poems for Reflection and Action

BY

S T Kimbrough, Jr.

FOREWORD BY

Charles Amjad-Ali

RESOURCE *Publications* · Eugene, Oregon

NATURE'S SORROWS AND NATURE'S JOYS
Poems for Reflection and Action

Resource Publications
An Imprint of Wipf and Stock Publishers
199 W. 8th Ave., Suite 3
Eugene, OR 97401

www.wipfandstock.com

PAPERBACK ISBN: 978-1-6667-6962-3
HARDCOVER ISBN: 978-1-6667-6963-0
EBOOK ISBN: 978-1-6667-6964-7

05/03/23

Contents

Section 3: Nature's Creatures

Section 4: Nature's Seasons

Winter

Spring

Summer

Foreword

This book of poems titled *Nature's Sorrows and Nature's Joys* begins with the tone of a requiem to Nature's Sorrows in section 1, before moving to Nature's Joys. The subtitle—*Poems of Reflection and Action*—is a demand for a *vita contemplativa* and a *vita activa*, which in themselves are imperative for human flourishing.

Greek philosophy dealt with a critical trinity of concerns which deeply linked ethics (*aretē*) with human flourishing (*eudaimonia*) and aesthetics (*aisthēsis*). We have a relative grasp of ethics/virtue and maybe even of aesthetics, but *eudaimonia* is another matter and it has been variously translated. It is not simply "happiness"— as in the Declaration of Independence's concept of the "pursuit of happiness"—but should be translated as the highest human good or overall human flourishing and entails the state or condition of "good spirit." The goal (*telos*) of philosophy, including ethics and political philosophy, was to contemplate what such "flourishing" really is, and then how to go about achieving it.

Aisthēsis was not simply about the concept of beauty and art, but more critically dealt with the very nature of taste and perception. Aesthetic ethics referred to the idea that human conduct and behavior ought to be governed by that which is beautiful and attractive, which were in themselves tied very closely with truth (*aletheia*). Thus there was a deep unity of aesthetics and ethics, and they were both reflected in our understanding of what is fair behavior. The word "fair" here reflects the double meaning of being attractive and morally acceptable.

The first chapter of Genesis narrates the creation story, reflecting all the cosmos in which we live and have our being. Critically, throughout this story, God admired God's own handiwork and creation, both aesthetically and ethically—thus the constant refrain that God saw what God had created and that "it was good" (Genesis 1:4, 10b, 12b, 18b, 21b, 25b, 31a; and 2:9b). If the human being is to have a role in it, it must also be for the maintenance of the good that this creation is. Yet we have violated this through our greed and gluttonous, uncontrolled consumptive patterns, which are not simply unethical but clearly also a deep impediment for flourishing.

S T has brought these three profound philosophical concerns to the fore in his poetry, focusing on environment through the aesthetics of poetry, through the ethics of human actions and ways of dwelling, and seeing in both the jeopardy to human life and even more to human flourishing, which is teleologically reflected throughout this collection dealing with nature.

In recent times I have taken the great commandment that "you shall love the Lord your God with all your heart, and with all your soul, and with all your mind, and with all your strength" (Mark 12:30), to entail the love also for the creation of this God, both human and nature. So, when I move to the second commandment, "You shall love your neighbor as yourself," I see nature as this overwhelming and all-encompassing neighbor—nature, the good creation. Nature then is a neighbor to be loved and cared for as myself, and any violation against that is also breaking the command, which opens the debate on a different scale. We have however not been environmentally responsible to this neighbor, but have treated nature purely as our consumptive storehouse which meets our gluttonous needs, rather than the good creation of God and our responsibility in it. This reminds me of 1 John 4:20, "Those who say, 'I love God', and hate their brothers or sisters, are liars; for those who do not love a brother or sister [nature and the earth] whom they have seen, cannot love God whom they have not seen." So in the caring and love of nature we are fully compliant with this commandment, and bring aesthetics, ethics and *eudaimonia* together.

The poems here, as I read them, play this imagination in great detail vis-a-vis flowers, seasons, animals, birds—all are taken as metaphors for the perception of creation so that nature's creatures and flowers become gateways to seeing the wonder, glory, and joy of creation and *eudaimonia*. The same is true of nature's seasons—each is given its own space, vis-a-vis winter, spring, summer, and autumn, each allowing a specific portal to look at, enjoy, and encapsulate, different sides of the same nature viewed through the prism of different weather patterns. This is S T's way of looking at nature, and he reveals this in the very first poem that appears in the introduction:

> One writes a poem or one paints,
> transforms what others may see,
> for artists know of no restraints
> to capture reality.

S T does not force anyone to view nature as he does, but invites us to have a transformative experience of what we see. He provides clues, *keyholes* if you will, to view nature, and takes us to the clues to see matters for ourselves and exercise our aesthetics without restraint. He encourages a multivalency to reality, which neither religious fundamentalism nor scientific certitude allows, but which is essential for human flourishing.

Charles Amjad-Ali, PhD, ThD

Introduction

In some of my other books of poetry that stress the importance of nature in our lives, I have concluded with sections on nature's demise.[1] One of the books reflects this concept in its title: *Nature's Final Curtain Call?* (2022). In the present volume, however, the first section is titled "Nature's Sorrow." I do not leave the concerns for the destruction of nature to the end. Instead of putting off addressing what is being done to nature through explicit human design, as well as neglect, this comes first.

Some may ask appropriately, "What difference can a poet's words make in correcting the paths of nature's destruction down which humankind is traveling?" Certainly words alone cannot save nature from destruction. Perhaps, however, artists can help to shape new understandings of human failure, as well as to shape new visions of hope.

Reality and Imagination

If skies should of their stars be stripped,
    if seas of waters be drained,
if sun and moon should be eclipsed,
    and visions of these restrained,
then poets, artists would be shorn
    of subjects, scenes to conceive,
the thoughts of great thinkers unborn,
    what would be left to believe?

---

1. See *A Seagull Lunch and Other Nature Poems (Save Our Planet)*, 2019. Also, *We Need Mountains: Poems on Creation Care and World Powers*, 2021.

Yes, wonder needs reality
    to feed imagination,
to paint perhaps an olive tree.
    What one sees has relation
to beauty or to harvest time,
    to olive oil's gestation,
to olive groves in a warm clime,
    to one's imagination.

The poets, artists help us see
    reality, but much more.
They capture its profundity
    through art that their gifts explore.
One writes a poem or one paints,
    transforms what others may see,
for artists know of no restraints
    to capture reality.

It is in this spirit that the current poems have been written.

The spinoff results of humankind's destruction of nature, be they the drastic results of climate change and global warming, the invisible presence of an overabundance of carbon dioxide and methane gases, destruction of rain forests, ongoing dependence on fossil fuels, etc., are becoming more and more urgent concerns.

We create the greenhouse gases,
    yes, I mean both you and me.
We can't see them, ev'n with glasses,
    but they're bold reality.

Carbon dioxide and methane,
    invisible though they be,
today science makes very plain
    aren't confined to industry.
. . .
The illnesses, deadening blows
    to nature and the earth,
the deaths caused now by what? Who knows?
    Another stillborn birth?

The worldwide plethora of refugees to be fed, housed, and given medical care is also overwhelming.

> The dreaded, shifting climate change,
> from valleys to each mountain range,
> leaves citizens and refugees
> distressed and without guarantees
> of aid from lands stretched to extremes
> with crises without end it seems.

While it is difficult for many citizens to grasp the diverse causes of nature's destruction, e.g., floods caused by enormous rainfall, and dry, parched earth with no hope of rain, scientists are providing the evidence that can help us correct some of human-kind's mistakes. It is foolish to ignore them. The reality that the existence of polar bears and sea turtles is threatened some may wish to ignore, but we must come

> to understand the need to act
> by every citizen of earth.
> Respect each scientific fact
> and know all species have their worth.

> Sea turtles' annual nesting sites,
> affected by the warming sand,
> could vanish and receive last rites,
> if we refuse to understand.

If there is hope at all amid earth's turmoil, it must be through action. Inaction hastens earth's demise.

> Naysayers keep their blinders on,
> refuse the facts to see
> and say to science, "Facts be gone!"
> and swoon in lethargy.

Hope lies within the human desire to retain the beauty of God's creation, but also to nurture all aspects of nature that sustain life. Across the planet earth farmers experience the loss of livelihood through lack of rain and parched earth. There is a daily threat of the death of refugees who cannot be properly fed, housed, or medically cared for. Children in hosts of unsanitary contexts die of dysentery and diseases for which there have long been vaccinations and cures. Of course, there are many organizations that address these issues, but it seems that the more they do, the more the needs increase. When one adds to these desperate needs the threat of natural disasters with their often total destruction of towns and villages, of crops and farmlands, one wonders whether there can be hope.

The remaining sections of poems address the joys of nature, which present and future generations could lose forever, if we do not creatively address nature's sorrows. Section 2, "Nature's Scenes," treats some of the joys of nature that every human being should experience, even if unaware of them.

> The wonders that creation shares
> on beaches, oceans wide;
> there's little that with them compares
> from streams to mountainside.

To be sure, creative ways must be found for children, youth, and adults trapped in city ghettos of concrete and asphalt to have such experiences.

The sky is there before us day after day, filled with wonders seen and unseen, morning, noon, and night. Do we pay attention? Here are some glimpses of what we may see.

> The night sky is a panoply
> of constellations' ecstasy.
> And all at once a shooting star
> expands the heav'ns' vast repertoire.

> . . .

> The moonlight glistening on the bay
> creates a sparkling, bright display.
> The sparkles gather and disperse
> as if they're scheduled to rehearse.

. . .

The sky today is pristine blue;
no birds or remnant moon is seen.
Nothing but blue comes into view;
the air again is fresh and clean.

Nature is filled with wonders that move and fill one's spirit. Our National Parks seek to preserve many of them, for which we should be thankful. Nature's art that withstands many genealogical ages still inspires us.

The jagged edges, crevices
awake a curious eye,
conveying diverse images:
a lion, butterfly.
A spectacle of rock and cloud
is this unusual park,
where quietly my head is bowed
from daylight until dark.

Section 3 addresses a few of "Nature's Creatures" that provide a special kind of nature joy. Yes, we rely on many animals and plants of the forest for food, but the poems in this section reflect particularly on the entertainment and fun many creatures provide us, if we are observant. The poems also reflect on creatures' responses within and to surrounding nature, for example, one sees how a mother sparrow protects her little ones amid a heavy wind.

When branches from the large oak tree
are blown by wind and swinging free,
the mother sparrow spreads her wings,
and then a warning song she sings.

The little ones to mother cling
lest oak tree branches toward them swing.
When suddenly the wind is past,
she knows that they are safe at last.

Section 4 views diverse aspects of nature's seasons: winter, spring, summer, and autumn.

From hemisphere to hemisphere
the seasons own the atmosphere
today and even year to year.

While the seasons are a constant in many parts of the world, the human experience of them is quite diverse from the equator to the North and South Poles. These seasonal aspects of nature bring disaster, sustenance, and many different forms of entertainment and joy. Farmers depend on the change of seasons for plowing, planting, and harvesting. Once again, however, the focus here tends toward the joys that the various seasons bring, joys it is to be hoped we will never lose because of nature's demise through intentional design or neglect:

spring waits it's turn for a new chance
for flowers' colors, blooms to dance,
to dance through meadows, mountains, hills
and offer up a thousand thrills.

Each season is unique with its own gifts of beauty and wealth of life-sustaining possibilities. Regardless of the season—

Of nature's beauty stand in awe;
on nature's beauty, yes, reflect.
Reflect on what you see and saw,
or you'll not know what to expect.
Drink in the beauty all around.
Give thanks that beauty you have found.

Section 5, "Nature's Flowers," reminds us of another aspect of nature that brings us immense joy. Flowers confront and surround us with incomparable beauty.

The yellow buttercups below,
wisteria up above,
azaleas, lilies in a row,
the iris kiss of love.

We do not always know what the experience of floral beauty means. We do not need to know. We know flowers inspire us and fill us with nature's joy.

> Monet's stunning, lovely flowers,
>   bright colored lily pads
> I love to observe for hours;
>   colors he adds and adds.

. . .

> You stop a moment, see his scenes,
>   then linger while entranced;
> you need not ask what each one means.
>   Your spirit danced and danced.

The multiple dimensions of "Nature Joy" fill our lives with wonder and ecstasy. Let us hope we are inspired to prevent their demise now and in the future. While we desperately need to preserve the aspects of nature that sustain life in many ways, the loss of "Nature Joy" would rob humankind of the wonder of nature's scenes, creatures, seasons, and flowers. Without them, what would we be?

Section 1

Nature's Sorrow

Nature's Sorrow

Today how saddened was the dawn,
  no seagulls swarmed the shore.
An oil-spill spread and most were gone,
  but some the oil-spill wore.

Their feathers now as black as coal,
  they stumbled, tumbled, fell.
How can one seagull pain console
  or free it from such hell?

They cannot search for fish or crab,
  or dive into the sea.
Their coat of feathers heavy, drab
  accents their misery.

They cannot move a step to fly
  or flutter weighted wings,
for drastic, human failure's why
  seagulls suffer such things.

Climate Collapse

What we today call climate change
    foreshadows a complete collapse,
when North Pole's fluctuating range
    of temperatures melts huge ice caps.

Antarctica's reached 40 Cs,
    disastrous for an arctic spring;
It too is losing by degrees
    the ice to which its creatures cling.

The polar bears and penguins soon
    may from this planet disappear,
while governments from morn till noon
    their GDPs prize and revere.

The rising heat waves humans cause
    the planet earth will soon destroy.
There's no time left to think, to pause;
    time's running out help to deploy.

Heal the Earth or Make It Bleed

If autumn this year can't arrive
    since temperatures still rise
to heights where plants cannot survive,
    crops' failures, no surprise.

The ground is parched, river beds dry,
    dead fish are strewn on shores;
there's no fresh water to get by
    and no fresh air outdoors.

Naysayers keep their blinders on,
    refuse the facts to see
and say to science, "Facts be gone!"
    and swoon in lethargy.

But slowly planet earth declines
    through negligence and greed.
It's humankind that hope defines:
    to heal or make it bleed.

Our Planet's Fate

Once more we learn our planet's fate,
    as temperatures higher climb.
Some people ask, "Is it too late,
    and is inaction our worst crime?"

Yes, lethargy's no help at all:
    as Africa endures more drought;
what island nations may befall
    with rising oceans, leaves no doubt.

Sea turtles' annual nesting sites,
    affected by the warming sand,
could vanish and receive last rites,
    if we refuse to understand,

to understand the need to act
    by every citizen of earth.
Respect each scientific fact
    and know all species have their worth.

The magnitude of nature's scheme
    the sciences still seek to learn.
Interdependence, nature's theme,
    we're very near to overturn.

A Greenhouse or Greenhouse Effect

A greenhouse on grandpa's farm
    was where I used to play.
It had its own special charm
    Flow'rs, veggies on display.

The fragrant smell of flowers
    filled all the greenhouse air,
and there I'd play for hours
    without a single care.

The earth's lower atmosphere
    has trapped warmth of the sun,
and slowly, slowly each year
    a warming trend's begun.

What then of greenhouse gases,
    that somehow must be checked,
for they affect the masses,
    a dire greenhouse effect?

The illnesses, deadening blows
    to nature and the earth.
Deaths caused by what now? Who knows?
    Another stillborn birth?

Rain, Rain, Go Away!

For many days torrential rains
have flooded all the central plains
till little of rich soil remains.

Erosion took it all away,
as gushing rivers on display
let roaring waters have their way.

The seedlings of a near tree farm
one thought the flood could do no harm;
their bright green rows lost all their charm.

There've never been such rains before;
one wonders if there's more in store.
What caused this terrible downpour?

Has global warming triggered this?
What is the cause? What did we miss?
It's no light matter to dismiss.

The rain has stopped and now bright sun
shines where the water used to run,
until one sees that there is none.

Now there is only sun-parched ground;
no fertile topsoil can be found,
and global warming's all around.

Tragic Chad

Decreasing rainfall now in Chad,
without a doubt the worst it's had,
leaves farmers all in spite of toil
no options to enrich the soil.
The fields cannot yield food and grain,
the barren fields will thus remain.
The farmers' loss of livelihood
cannot for nation Chad be good.
The dreaded, shifting climate change,
from valleys to each mountain range,
leaves citizens and refugees
distressed and without guarantees
of aid from lands stretched to extremes
with crises without end, it seems.
But climate change is no charade,
so, will the world the Chadians aid?

A Carbon Footprint

My bookshelf holds a cast footprint
    of my son at one year old.
But there was never any hint
    of what was yet to be told:

a carbon footprint each one leaves;
    one is left by everyone.
But on this planet who believes
    that it is a smoking gun?

We create the greenhouse gases,
    yes indeed, both you and I.
We can't see them, ev'n with glasses;
    they're there, one cannot deny.

Carbon dioxide and methane,
    invisible though they be,
today science makes very plain
    aren't confined to industry.

The molded footprint of my son
    has a matching carbon print
and it could be of anyone;
    but it's there, we need no hint.

Think of the Children

For coal, there's dreadful strip mining;
for wood, forests are declining;
for natural gas, there is fracking;
of crude oil, soon we'll be lacking.

Strip Mother Earth of life's sources,
by thoughtless destructive forces,
we'll have no way to heat our homes,
though we're as smart as Sherlock Holmes.

There'll be no way to cook our food,
and power-driven tools no good.
Electro-energy won't last,
with power plants things of the past.

Just so there is enough for you
won't help your children to get through
the worst disasters to be seen—
no air to breathe, water that's clean.

Would-Be Springtime

At times late winter's warmth may fool
    the trees and flow'rs to bloom.
And yet we know this isn't the rule,
    for winter may resume.

This would-be springtime's a delight,
    though nature is confused.
The tulip-tree blooms, what a sight,
    though nature's not bemused.

The Mother-Nature cycles bring
    her seasons in due course:
the winter snows and flow'rs of spring,
    and harvests, our food source.

But global warming now disrupts
    the seasons as earth turns,
and methane gas slowly corrupts,
    and nature's balance spurns.

A Morning in the Woods

How overcast the morning sky,
    how calm the atmosphere.
Low-hanging clouds are passing by,
    no chance that they will clear.

Outside my window trees are bare,
    for autumn leaves are gone.
The quiet valley seems in prayer:
    may morrow bring clear dawn.

Amid the quiet the woods seem
    at peace by morning's light,
and yet unknown to eyes they teem
    with life that's out of sight.

Beneath the fallen leaves one finds
    the busy world of worms,
of insects, bugs of many kinds;
    it seems the earth there squirms.

They're all essential to the woods
    and their ongoing life.
They are essential forest foods,
    especially for wildlife.

If overcast or clear the day,
    life in the woods goes on,
unless we stand in nature's way:
    then her life's blood's withdrawn.

Through fracking, fossil fuel search,
    with methane gas results,
the woods *we* very fast besmirch,
    the *we,* so-called adults.

Or forest fires through carelessness
    destroy the forest's floor
and forest life is motionless;
    and forest life's no more.

Lost Loveliness

In contrast to earth's loveliness,
there is the oceans' plastic mess:
the refuse floats from shore to shore,
ev'n after cleanups there is more.
There's garbage dumped from giant ships,
and oceans' balance quickly flips
from living food farms that feed fish
to miles of trash no one would wish.
Then add the damage of oil spills
that cause sea fowls the gravest ills.
There's nuclear waste, a drastic threat
from plants with breaches, deadly yet.
Who wants to swim along a beach
that shows gross signs of nature's breach?
The cleanup efforts can't keep pace
with damage of pollution's race.
As science knocks on every door,
with facts that shock us all the more,
they tell us humans are to blame,
yet science remedies can name.
When we don't heed the proven facts,
then nature's beauty fades, contracts.

Nature's Displeasure

Another dam diverts the flow
of water from a river bed
that it began centuries ago,
but forest life it has left dead.
Now drowned beneath a giant lake
which we are told's progress we need.
The dam makes Mother Nature ache,
while cities, "Electric pow'r!" plead.

For eco-consciousness we pray
that urban, rural engineers,
through science find a helpful way
and genuine concern appears,
for nature's *and* for humans' needs
to coexist successfully,
which must be seen in actual deeds.
If not, what is our destiny?

Nature's Violence

Though nature can evoke great joy,
its violence can life destroy.
Its cyclones, hurricanes, typhoons
strike mornings, nights, and afternoons.
They care not what lies in their wake;
their giant rumblings make earth quake.
Add global warming's damage, harm,
a terrifying new alarm.
It makes these storms ev'n more intense.
Are we then left with no defense?
As city homes are washed away
by sudden rains that came their way,
and typhoons rip up planted fields
of rice that never will show yields,
a mother mourns her firstborn son
as nature's violence has won.

Thinking of Turkey and Syria

As buildings crumble, one hears cries
    of mothers, fathers, families.
An elderly grandmother dies,
    no burial formalities.

An earthquake aftershock brings down
    a tower teetering in the wind.
There's little left within the town
    with people under rubble pinned.

The power of nature strikes at life,
    a power inexplicable.
And husband, father, children, wife
    are buried—it's unthinkable.

Though humankind tries to prepare
    for nature's vast destructive power,
it strikes when we are unaware
    and threatens lives hour upon hour.

Though scientists can give us clues
    to some disasters on the way,
some push away such dreadful news,
    but nature's force they can't delay.

Section 2

Nature's Joy

Nature's Joy

Today how cheerful was the dawn,
　　as robins started to sing.
They chirped and skipped across my lawn,
　　then all at once they took wing.

If you'd like joy to fill your day,
　　let nature entertain you.
Your spirit it will swing and sway,
　　invigorate each sinew.

A deer, an owl, a small red fox,
　　an amaryllis in bloom,
a rosebush, and a field of phlox,
　　a peacock spreading its plume.

Yes, nature will your soul enthrall,
　　just glimpse the sunshine at play.
In summer, winter, spring, and fall;
　　let nature's joy have its way.

Morning Delight

The sky at dawn was snowy-white
    and decked with clouds of ivory.
But soon these clouds passed out of sight,
    blue patches were their rivalry.

As white clouds were surpassed by blue
    by winds that seemed at lightning speed,
an airplane quickly came in view,
    as if it were from darkness freed.

I marveled at how rich the blue
    appeared amid the sun's bright rays.
As wonder of this moment grew,
    my soul rejoiced with nature's praise.

The Morning Mist

Above the waves a cloudy mist,
 as far as eyes can see,
the far horizon lip has kissed
 the sky and then the sea.

It patiently awaits sunrise
 when warmth and bright sunlight
will dissipate before your eyes
 the mist as it takes flight.

And then as if it owns the scene,
 the sunlight starts the day;
some surfaces have a bright sheen,
 while others light defray.

The wonders that creation shares
 on beaches, oceans wide;
there's little that with them compares
 from streams to mountainside.

Yet I'll explore creation's gifts
 throughout this earthbound realm,
perhaps as well its seabound-cliffs;
 such wonders overwhelm.

A Jersey Shore Sunrise

The sunrise at the Jersey Shore—
I want to see it more and more.
It glistens on the ocean waves,
and every downcast moment saves.
Its brilliant orange fantasy
along the beach, a thrill to see.
A seagull silhouette wings past
as if in a large painting cast.
The sun then rises to new heights
between the clouds now silver, white.
Would that each day could so begin
for sunrise makes me smile within.

A Sunset's Charm

A stream of orange, fire-like blaze,
    spreads quickly through the sunset sky.
I stand in utmost awe and gaze
    at color-bursts that flood the eye.
Suspended clouds at once are trimmed
    in pink, and gray, and purple hues,
breathtaking sights as daylight dimmed,
    more stunning than the landscape views.

Mid streams of forest-fire like flames
    the daylight blue begins to wane.
As twilight nature's beauty frames,
    this vision will with me remain.
I look around and turn my head,
    the sun then ushers in the night.
Away this pristine painting sped
    but not without divine delight.

Evening Calm

Two swans drift quietly along
upon a stream at evening time.
Across the calm a sweet birdsong
accompanies this scene sublime.

Behind the swans six little ones
are drifting in a single line.
They move along as the stream runs,
a charming, peaceful, calm design.

Six little cygnets, as they're called,
begin to wear a new white coat.
The watcher stands entranced, enthralled
to see this family afloat.

Their nest nearby, they disappear,
as parent swans their cygnets keep
from danger, threats, as well as fear,
that they may have a peaceful sleep.

Nighttime Skies

When starlight fills the nighttime skies,
at times it's veiled by clouds' disguise,
which also covers moonbeam glow,
perhaps in winter veiled by snow.

But when the clouds are drawn away
by winds, we see the Milky Way;
we see Orion and Pisces,
or Leo, Virgo, and Aries.

The night sky is a panoply
of constellations' ecstasy.
And all at once a shooting star
expands the heav'ns' vast repertoire,

a repertoire of planets, moons,
and stars evoking lovers' swoons.
A thing of wonder to delight
creation's glory every night.

Another Bleak and Dreary Day

Another bleak and dreary day
    looms on the dark horizon,
and flocks of birds their fright display,
    for there's no sun that's risin'.

The temperature is colder
    than happens this time of year.
I can feel it in my shoulder,
    the pain feels sharp as a spear.

Perhaps it's best to go inside
    where there is no wind nor cold.
Here comes the rain, so I decide
    to run before floods unfold.

Unexpected Surprise

The moonlight glistening on the bay
creates a sparkling, bright display.
The sparkles gather and disperse
as if they're scheduled to rehearse.
They ride upon the ripples, waves,
some disappear into the caves
that line the rocky, jagged shore
that by bright moonlight I explore.
I wonder if they're cold and damp
with places dry enough to camp?
By moonlight I cannot resist
to see of what these caves consist.
One simple pass-by in my boat,
I look in and I see afloat
a boat like mine with a bright light
and what I see is quite a sight:
on one large wall I see outlined
some animals, not well defined:
are they a cow, a fox, a deer?
One wonders who it was lived here.
Were these line-drawings perhaps drawn
by ancient peoples long since gone?
Or are they just a modern prank
drawn on this cave wall dark and dank?
Indeed I would like to know more;
I'll come back one day to explore.

The Sky

The sky today is pristine blue,
    no birds or remnant moon is seen.
Nothing but blue comes into view;
    the air again is fresh and clean.

It has the feeling of "just made,"
    as though creation's just begun
with sky-blue that can never fade,
    made brighter by the glowing sun.

O sky of purest, pristine blue,
    you offer all a morning kiss
with such enticing, stunning hue,
    such sky, such joy, such perfect bliss.

The Sun and Moon

The sunbeams just like sleek moonbeams
    cast shadows where they will.
A moonbeam like a sunbeam seems
    at times just to stand still.

Though they're alike in many ways,
    they are quite different too.
The warmth and power of sun's bright rays
    contrast the moon's soft hue.

Both are romantic in their ways
    as fits each lover's taste.
Some share caresses mid sunrays,
    some moonbeams never waste.

The Forest Green

The beauty of the forest green
where city children have not been,
and city gangs have never seen,
can transform spirits, change one's view
of nature that one never knew,
for one sees life, the world brand new.
To touch a tree leaf, see a fox,
to see unusual streams and rocks,
or shepherds calling in their flocks,
can children change for their lives long,
can help them see where they belong
within a world of nature's song.
This song has strains for all to sing;
it matters not what gifts we bring—
from folk songs to a highland fling.
The forest green awakes the soul
with sounds a spirit can console,
with solitude from pole to pole.

A Nearby Lake

I saw a lake all trimmed in green;
its ripples had a silver sheen.
Its color was a blue-like hue,
and trees along the shore were few.
A motor boat created waves
that vanished in the shoreline caves.
A young boy with a fishing pole
sat quietly with but one goal.
He watched intently for a strike
of catfish, trout, but not of pike.
Across the lake a large black bear
caught breakfast and the young boy's stare.
The morning air was fresh and clean;
I sat and mused on what I'd seen.

Nature's Décor

How brightly shines my holly tree,
    each leaf in sunlight beams.
Its berries, red, the apogee
    of nature's color schemes.

Each time that I look out my door
    and see it standing there,
I'm thankful for nature's décor,
    a splendid sight and rare.

Arches National Park

The regal arches made of stone
    reach upward to the sky.
Their upward reach is not alone
    for gravity is nigh.
The arched peaks with their anchored feet,
    that hold up tons of rock,
form Utah's landscape, nature's feat,
    withstanding age's clock.

The jagged edges, crevices
    awake a curious eye,
conveying diverse images:
    a lion, butterfly.
A spectacle of rock and cloud
    is this unusual park,
where quietly my head is bowed
    from daylight until dark.

It feels like desert solitaire,
    perhaps like Walden Pond.
One sees a giant ogre rare,
    knows not how to respond.
Is it a stone god standing there?
    One asks, "What lies behind
such beauty soaring in the air?"
    It's awe we humbly find.

Mysterious Moments

When dune-grass twinkles in moonlight,
  sand-pebble sparkles grace the sand,
they shine like armor of a knight
  with shield, lance, sword, all three at hand.

The pounding waves seem like a foe
  the mystic knight prepares to fight.
As each one crests, the wind dares blow
  as strong as from a giant's might.

The knight, so valiant, takes a stand,
  as mist envelopes the tense scene.
As if one waved a magic hand,
  the mist is gone, nothing is seen.

Nature's Pleasure

The willows wave in the breeze,
their branches swaying with ease.
The soft morning light breaks through
embraced by gentle sky-blue.
A humming bird feasts on blooms
whose sweet nectar it consumes.
A robin pecks at the ground,
with hope a worm will be found.
A rabbit peaks from a bush
and looks like it needs a push.
A squirrel is trying to rob
some bird seed, though a tough job.
A chipmunk's waiting to see
if acorns fall from a tree.
All this is outside my door,
yet nature's pleasure is more!
So why wait inside? Go out,
for pleasure's waiting, no doubt!

World Beauty

Around the world there's loveliness:
seas, rivers, trees, and wilderness,
the Hudson River's steady flow
'neath hanging cliffs at sunset's glow.
There's fog 'round San Francisco Bay
that doesn't seem to go away.
In Kenya, Maasai Mara's length,
the hippos, lions show their strength.
In East Malaysia skies are blue
above Kota Kinabalu.
In Vietnam there's the Mekong,
that's longer than sea-girt Hong Kong.
Sequoias on the western coast,
are worthy California's boast.
Across plains of Mongolia,
you won't find a magnolia.
The Rhine's bewitching Loreley,
and Switzerland's thick snow-filled sky,
Jerusalem's Al Aksa mosque,
in Paris there's a food kiosk,
in Rome there is St. Peter's dome,
thus beauty's everywhere at home.
Such beauty greets us traveling on,
the world's a grand phenomenon.

What a Morning

The blaze of morning sunlight
makes morning shadows take flight.
Its brightness burns away dawn,
as if the night shades were drawn.
An airplane's trail in the sky
suddenly catches my eye.
A flock of chimney sweeps flies
up, down, around at sunrise.
The wind wafts softly through trees
with whistling sounds that reprise
like piccolos in concert
with tunes as sweet as dessert.
The morning's here, what a thrill,
exhibiting nature's skill.

A Forest Bare

I looked out through the forest bare,
    the tree leaves all were gone.
I saw what I'd not known was there,
    as sunlight rose at dawn.

A tiny cabin roof peeked through
    the stalwart standing pines.
The shiny tin roof of bright blue
    was one of many signs,

the signs that autumn long was past,
    the pines the only green.
The summer flowers did not last,
    nowhere could they be seen.

The forest floor was dark and vast,
    as streams of sunlight made
strange images, and light it cast
    turned brightness into shade.

I saw some forest creatures rush
    across a fallen log;
a rabbit jumped behind a bush,
    and out jumped a big frog.

O forest bare, how I delight
    to see what I can't see
when lovely leaves keep out of sight
    the life behind each tree.

A Waterfall

A waterfall's incessant stream
    of water that's cascading down,
sometimes exerts force quite extreme,
    yet looks like nature's evening gown.

It's elegant, and yet a force
    with power to crush all that's beneath.
Or it's a gentle water source,
    as lovely as a bridal wreath.

The Charming Rain

The rain glides down a window pane
in one continuous rippling skein.
It changes everything in sight,
some things move left, others move right.
A passing car jumps up and down,
the gliding ripples turn it 'round.
The branches of a large oak tree
look like an octopus at sea.
Its arms flail this way and then that,
some form large circles, some are flat.
The rippling water moves them 'round
till numerous images abound.
A baby eel goes slithering by,
while sheets of snow fall from the sky.
My, how the rain can entertain
by gliding down a window pane.

Evening Wonder

To go for a stroll
along a broad knoll,
in the fresh evening air, how good for the soul.
At close of the day,
as light fades away
it seems that the world all around wants to pray.

One moment I pause
and not without cause,
for bright evening stars give creation applause.
For you, and for me
what wonders we see:
each river, each brook, every bird, and each tree.

What solace, what peace,
what quiet release,
at twilight's soft light how the shadows increase.
As I stand quite still,
I'm filled with a thrill
from soothing, pure sounds of a sweet whippoorwill.

What Delight Each Night Is Mine

As the evening stars appear,
　　heaven's wonders multiply,
though so distant, some are clear
　　like constellations in the sky.
Would that I could travel there,
to the heavens, where, O where?

What delight each night is mine,
　　Venus, evening star so bright,
joins the planets' glow and shine,
　　as the world turns night by night.
As it turns, perceptions change,
stars and planets rearrange.

Yet, what order in the sky
　　far beyond what I can see,
far beyond the human eye:
　　wonders of a galaxy!
Thanks to science for the view:
wonders that we never knew.

Section 3

Nature's Creatures

A Change of Scene

A young deer came out of the wood
and silently a moment stood.
Its regal stature caught my eye,
joined by a magpie from the sky.
The magpie did not make a sound,
while perched unnoticed on the ground.
It was indeed a curious sight—
a deer so still, no bird in flight.
As if they froze in time and space,
no movement of the two took place.
A sudden dog-bark changed the scene;
in seconds neither one was seen.

A Fawn at Dawn

A blue-hued fog arose at dawn
    across a jasmine-colored lake.
Within its haze appeared a fawn
    so young it's thin legs seemed to shake.

At water's edge bent down its head,
    as if about to take a drink,
but suddenly with legs outspread
    it teetered slowly on the brink,

the brink of slowly falling down
    and landing squarely in the lake.
It looked just like a circus clown;
    the soothing drink had to forsake.

A Garden Squirrel

A squirrel with a white-tinged tail
    surveys the garden scene.
It seems he surveys each detail,
    a daily squirrel routine.

He sees a feeder hanging there,
    that's for the birds, he knows,
and yet it is his daily dare
    this purpose to oppose.

He jumps atop the feeder post,
    his agile skills to show,
then shakes the feeder loose, almost
    till some seeds downward flow.

He springs high up into the air,
    then lands with four paws spread,
and ready other squirrels to dare
    at his feast to be fed.

A Morning Fray

A dolphin sprang into the air,
so close that it gave me a scare.
Our boat was tipped, rocked to and fro,
so near the dock I did not know
if our small boat would flip and crash,
because of such a giant splash.
Just as the water calmed a bit,
perhaps it was with dolphin wit
the dolphin soared, then like a bomb,
its mighty crash, what could becalm?
Our boat was thrown against the dock;
we need not fear that it would rock.
The bow was wedged between two posts,
as if lodged there by dolphin ghosts.
We saw the dolphin swim away,
as if quite joyfully to say,
"Goodbye, my friends, I've had my fun."
And so our day had just begun.

A Mother Sparrow

A giant oak with new green leaves
has branches reaching to the eaves,
the eaves where sparrows made a nest,
and little sparrows now find rest.

When branches from the large oak tree
are blown by wind and swinging free,
the mother sparrow spreads her wings,
and then a warning song she sings.

The little ones to mother cling
lest oak tree branches toward them swing.
When suddenly the wind is past,
she knows that they are safe at last.

An Unlucky Bird

Across the water skimmed a bird,
    a seagull or a pelican?
A wave crashed and my sight was blurred,
    just as the bird's loud squawk began:

Mist cleared, it was a pelican
    that dived to catch its morning meal.
Behaving as these wise birds can,
    it caught a writhing, struggling eel.

But suddenly it let it go;
    I guess it much preferred a fish.
It dived again, quite in the know,
    and up it came with one big swish.

Its beak was filled with a sea trout;
    I wondered if it could hold on.
The fish was struggling, turned about,
    and in a second it was gone.

The bird unlucky, lost its prey,
    and flew to a large post to perch.
I looked once more, then turned away;
    I left the bird to its next search.

Face to Face

A squirrel and a cardinal bird
    are standing face to face.
They stare and neither one seems stirred
    the other to displace.

Then quickly a chipmunk appears
    and starts a threatening chase.
The bird flies off, squirrel disappears,
    then neither's face to face.

The Rabbit and the Toad

I saw a rabbit by moonlight,
    its eyes unusually glowed.
It stood unmoved, displayed no fright
    till all at once it met a toad.

The toad jumped forward, then stood still,
    the rabbit's tail abruptly flinched.
But neither meant the other ill,
    yet each was in its place entrenched.

I slowly turned my flashlight on
    and shined it on the rabbit, toad,
and in a second both were gone,
    one in the bush, one down the road.

A Seagull Paradise

With rising of the early dawn
    my eyes to seagulls are drawn;
        they soar out of my sight.
Will they again today be seen,
    create yet another scene
        before the shades of night?

This need not be a prime concern,
    tomorrow I will discern
        that seagulls will appear.
They're fishing at the earliest hour,
    on the beach they scour and scour,
        some scrounging round the pier.

How they survive is quite a feat;
    their daily task: what to eat,
        to find what will suffice.
In ocean waters how they dive
    to catch a meal to survive,
        a seagull's paradise.

Section 4

Nature's Seasons

Winter

Clinging Snow

My yucca plant's long, pointed leaves,
    outside my window pane,
are filled with snow, like long, white sleeves,
    and do they entertain!
I watch and watch the clinging snow:
    how long will it stay there?
With temperature's above zero,
    I guess, I'll stare and stare.

Foreboding Snow

The street is filled with snow on snow,
which fell when temperatures were low.
Though most reporters snow foretold,
some folks found such reports too bold.
For those who left their plants outside,
it's no surprise that some have died.
And some folks paid a higher price
and wrecked their cars on slick, black ice.
But children's fascination rose
when they put on a snowman's nose.
And what a joy to make snow-cream,
for children it's a winter dream.
So, snow bodes danger and great fun,
and common sense from everyone.

Gentle Snowfall

Without hesitation snow falls,
falls gently on crevices, walls.
Its blanket of soft glistening white
makes cities and hills a delight.
When snow falls, life's at a calm pace.
One walks, does not join in the race
of automobiles, giant trucks
and traffic that oft self-destructs.
Enjoy the snow-pace for the time
as snow gently falls in your clime.
Though winter storms are rarely kind,
a gentle snowfall calms the mind.

Outside My Window

Outside my window there's a tree
    whose limbs are bending low;
each winter it is hardly free,
    from rain, or hail, or snow.

It seems to offer anguished prayer
    to every passer-by:
"Can no one see my sad despair?
    Does no one wonder why

"my limbs are just about to break?
    Will no one trim them back?
Does no one see how much I ache,
    and how much help I lack?"

Sometimes in nature there's a sign,
    like long, long limbs that bend,
to show us nature's own design
    of how it needs to mend.

Sledding Time

The snow came down again today
    and painted all the landscape white.
Though it's too thin for Grandpa's sleigh,
    the snow for grandkids is just right.

They built an igloo tall and deep,
    then crawled inside, two girls, a boy.
They acted like they'd gone to sleep,
    for fun their Grandpa to annoy.

He called out, "How about a sled?"
    That ended their sleep pantomime.
Then Grandpa said, "Get out of bed!
    Come on! Come on! It's sledding time!"

Red Cheeks

A little sparrow fluffs its wings,
    as I walk slowly by,
and with a chirp it sings and sings
    as snow falls from the sky.
The more it fluffs its wings the snow
    lands lightly on my face,
and little does the sparrow know
    my red cheeks show the trace,

the trace indeed of ice-cold snow,
    that lands upon my cheeks.
With temperatures that are so low,
    we may have snow for weeks.
I'll brush away the ice-cold snow
    and go inside to warm.
My cheeks will then lose their red glow,
    and I'll be free from harm.

A Sparkling Willow Tree

An ice storm turned a willow tree
into a sparkling jubilee.
Each slender leaf now rimmed with ice
projects an ice-trimmed paradise.
As sunlight strikes each charming leaf,
I'm struck with utter unbelief,
for moments I stand with fixed gaze
at diamond-like, bright, twinkling rays
exploding in an atmosphere,
which at this moment I find here.
What glorious unexpected art
of which I'm suddenly a part!

What Beauty

The landscapes dusted white with snow
by moonlight cast a crystal glow.
The sky is clear with beaming stars.
Perhaps I'll catch a glimpse of Mars.
A shooting star whisks through the sky.
I make a wish and think, Oh my!
A wish for anything seems strange,
with beauty's overwhelming range,
a range the universe extends,
a range that seems to have no ends.
Were I an astronaut a while,
I'd see on earth a new profile
of beauty, wonder from afar,
as if I were a circling star.
But for the moment I'm content
with beauty on this continent,
where landscapes dusted white with snow
are beauty I delight to know.

Winter's Last Gasp

As snowflakes gently float on air,
a robin wings its love affair
with winter's softly, wafting wind,
first to ascend then to descend.
In April winter's final gasp
releases its ungentle grasp,
spring waits its turn for a new chance
for flowers' colors, blooms to dance,
to dance through meadows, mountains, hills
and offer up a thousand thrills.

Spring

Nature's Holy Grail

When the winter snows are gone,
spring appears to carry on.
Snow white fields depart at last,
winter's biting winds are past.
Gone are freezing temperatures,
welcome are all spring's allures:
sweet, sweet sounds of birds in song,
trickling brooks that run along.
Roadside flowers in full bloom
share their fragrant spring perfume.
On the sides of rolling hills
one sees yellow daffodils.
Spring is nature's Holy Grail;
joy on joy not to curtail!

A Sign of Spring

The royal-purple iris bloom
　　adorns my garden for it's spring;
however, one cannot assume
　　that first blooms spring will bring.

I've seen these blooms with flakes of snow
　　perched on their gentle lips,
when Ol' Man Winter lets you know
　　he would springtime eclipse.

Then comes the wind to dust away
　　the snowflakes clinging there.
This warmer breeze of spring's new day
　　with winter will not share.

The Atmosphere of Springtime

The atmosphere of springtime
    embraces meadows, and hills,
as winter's snowy, cold clime
    recedes with its ice and chills.

The smell of springtime flowers,
    whose fragrance fills the spring air,
gives me pleasure for hours,
    as if it's nature's spring prayer.

Her prayer of seasonal change
    gives hope that nature renews.
Each valley, each mountain range
    is nature's seasonal muse.

Colors of Spring

The colors of a brand new spring
from San Francisco to Beijing
care not the least for strident views
of left and right that make the news.
Care not if Moscow bombs Ukraine,
for blooming flowers won't refrain
from opening blooms when springtime comes
with multi-colored, blooming mums.
The flowers' colors do not care
if war is here or war is there.
They show themselves a charmed design
on Scottish hillsides, on the Rhine.
Unless destroyed themselves by war,
all nature's colors hopes restore.

Nature's Beauty

On rolling hills of newborn spring
    when colors often turn to green,
the village children dance a fling,
    as heather's on the hillsides seen.
The little chipmunks dance and play,
while field mice tumble in the hay.

The meadow clover blooms turn pink;
    the yellow sunflow'r blooms are bright.
Such beauty makes me stop and think,
    but lest I think, two birds alight,
as if to say, "First just enjoy:
like children, ev'ry girl and boy."

Of nature's beauty stand in awe;
    on nature's beauty, yes, reflect.
Reflect on what you see and saw,
    or you'll not know what to expect.
Drink in the beauty all around.
Give thanks that beauty you have found.

Spring Rains

The rains that poured from heaven last night
were Mother Nature's spring delight.

Brown grass will once again turn green,
and meadow flowers once more be seen.

Bare limbs of trees will burst with signs
of life from nature's own designs.

The rains turn planted fields' fresh soil
to life after the farmers' toil.

The sprigs of corn blades soon peek through,
the wheat fields know just what to do,

for water's life for Mother Earth;
it gives each living thing new birth.

We welcome spring rain once again,
our lives to nourish and sustain.

Springtime Delights

I look and springtime's everywhere,
a redbud tree, a Bradford pear
display their colors as they bloom,
dismissing much of winter's gloom.
Just down the street a tulip tree
is bursting with a color spree
of pink and white, what sheer delight
in sunlight or by night's moonlight.
The apple trees beyond my lawn
burst forth with deep pink blooms at dawn.
Magnolia trees will wait awhile;
their fragrant blooms will make me smile.
O springtime's a delight to me,
a smorgasbord of colors free.

Summer

Summer Fun

My first attempt to waterski
    took place when I was just sixteen.
Towline in hand I bent each knee
    and hoped my take-off would be clean.

The pilot of the boat yelled, "Start!"
    The motor revved, the boat took off;
I thought it would pull me apart,
    I sank into a water trough.

And then as if shot from a gun,
    my waterskies just skimmed along.
Across the lake I raced, what fun;
    I thought that nothing could go wrong.

Just then another boat whizzed by.
    Its waves made me shift left, then right.
I tried my best strength to apply,
    but fell; it was no pretty sight.

One ski flew this way, one flew that,
    I should have let the towline go;
held on too long, then landed flat.
    I'm sure folks knew—I'm not a pro.

Summer Sky

The sky today is pristine blue,
    no bird nor remnant moon is seen.
There's only blue comes into view;
    the air I breathe is fresh and clean.

There is the feeling of "just made,"
    as though creation's just begun
and sky-blue that can never fade,
    made brighter by the glowing sun.

O sky of purest, pristine blue;
    enriching beauty to my eyes,
your all-enticing, wondrous hue,
    indeed is a creation prize.

Sunlight Starts the Day

Above the waves a cloudy mist,
 as far as eyes can see,
the far horizon lip has kissed,
 the sky and then the sea.

It patiently awaits sunrise
 when warmth and bright sunlight
will dissipate before my eyes
 the mist as it takes flight.

And then, as if it rules the scene,
 the sunlight starts the day.
Some surfaces have a bright sheen
 while others light defray.

A Sunset's Charm

A stream of orange, fire-like blaze,
  spreads quickly through the sunset sky.
I stand in utmost awe and gaze
  at color-bursts that flood the eye.
Suspended clouds at once are trimmed
  in pink, and gray, and purple hues,
breathtaking sights as daylight dimmed,
  more stunning than the landscape views.

Mid streams of forest-fire like flames
  the daylight blue begins to wane.
As twilight nature's beauty frames,
  this evening wonder will remain.
I look around and turn my head,
  the sun then ushers in the night.
Away this pristine painting sped
  but leaves its own divine delight.

The Magic of the Summer Wind

The summer wind blew through her hair,
    a silhouette against blue sky
of elegance beyond compare,
    each brunette strand lifted so high.
That moment etched upon my mind
    remains a constant memory
of love and beauty both combined.
    No moment could more tender be.

So, summer wind, I'm in your debt
    for love and beauty both revealed.
I saw within that silhouette
    the love that in my heart was sealed.
Though brunette strands have turned to gray,
    the summer wind wafts through them still.
The silhouette yet holds its sway,
    and memory's vision's still a thrill.

Sunlight's Wonders

What contrast to the winter snow,
the sun is putting on a show.
O how it sparkles on the lawn,
so dew-besprinkled since the dawn!
Its beams are dancing down a lane
as orange rays cloak the terrain.
A yellow buttercup unfolds,
a sign of what the future holds:
the wondrous beauty of a day
when nature's sunlight comes to play.

A Summer Race

The sailboats poised before the race,
    await the starting gun.
Which one today will set the pace?
    They're off, the race begun.

Each one received the day's race course,
    and tacks a long zigzag.
The wind alone's the power source,
    so strong no sail can sag.

Today the wind is steady, strong.
    The spinnakers are full.
The sailboats seem to glide along,
    as racers fiercely pull.

Then all at once a sudden gust
    thrusts one boat to one side.
The sailors quickly knew they must
    stretch, lean out, lean out wide.

Their weight it seems was just enough
    to save them from the drink.
Disaster this time they'd rebuff,
    though they'd been on its brink.

The sudden gust they did not know
    had put them far ahead.
Across the finish line they'd go,
    past all the boats they'd sped.

Autumn

A Welcome Exchange

How brisk the air and warm the sun.
I think that summer's on the run.

Perhaps for just a few days more
the summer heat will fall ignore.

But then as nature shuts a door,
comes autumn's season to adore.

The change to cooler temp'ratures,
fall colors have their own allures.

The many-colored forest trees
my eyes take in with pleasant ease.

The morning, cool breeze on my face,
a waft of gentleness and grace,

makes me so thankful for the change:
the fall for summer to exchange.

Refreshing Autumn

To summer's heat I'll say goodbye,
with autumn's cool breeze breathe a sigh.

The sigh is for a change of mood,
for autumn's colors, gratitude!

I see leaves' hues change within days,
their gold highlighted by sun rays.

I watch the squirrels store their cache
of nuts and acorns, winter's stash.

The sense of change—summer to fall
from earliest childhood I recall.

In mounds of fallen leaves I'd play
with friends; what joy was on display.

Each autumn revives young days past.
What joy these memories still last.

No Match for Autumn

Below my house's wooden eaves
I noticed all the golden leaves—
again in autumn one believes.

I feel how brisk the morning air,
at hillside colors how I stare.
At evening a cool breeze is there.

I thought a jacket's what I need
and put one on with undue speed.
It was an error, I'll concede.

The perspiration down my back
made quite a stream easy to track
that tried the cool breeze to hijack.

Off went the jacket with dispatch
so evening's coolness I might catch;
for autumn breezes there's no match.

The Life of Autumn Leaves

I watch the wind dance with the leaves
    that grace a large oak tree,
one large brown leaf sways upward, weaves
    then circles quietly.
The oak tree's trunk is very large;
    the leaf circles just twice
before the wind makes one last charge
    that keeps it from the ice.

As autumn leaves turn gold and brown,
    cold winds turn dew to ice.
The leaf is ready to come down,
    but ice does not entice.
The leaf knew stories of past leaves
    trapped deep in ice and snow.
And when it thinks of them it grieves;
    they had no place to go.

But other leaves were free to fly
    on autumn winds here, there.
Some autumn leaves have flown so high,
    they've soared o'er famed Red Square.
Imagine leaves that are so free,
    they reach the Amazon.
What wondrous sights the leaves can see
    as they fly on and on.

An Autumn Dream

Tree leaves are turning through our town
    as autumn colors start their change.
The wind wafts through them red, gold, brown;
    it's nature's winsome, charmed exchange.

My friend's house which is painted white
    Is now embraced with golden trim
from oak and elm trees, what a sight,
    the colors shine on every limb!

And down the street my friend named Joe
    lives in a house where redbud trees
have turned to yellow, now aglow
    in sunlight and a dancing breeze.

O autumn, nature's color scheme
    that graces hillsides, village streets,
we see now mirrored in a stream;
    the season its reflection meets.

An Autumn Ball

The trees dressed for the autumn dance
of colors soon are given the chance.
The autumn breezes start their sway
so red, bronze, yellow, brown, and gray
join in each waltz and each fox-trot.
By autumn winds they had been taught,
along with samba and tango
and other dances long ago.
We're all invited to the hall—
to Mother Nature's autumn ball.

Autumn's Prize

The trees before my house turn red;
in spring they will be green instead.

Behind my house some leaves are brown;
above them bronze ones form a crown.

The bronze ones run around a vine
with yellow leaves, then intertwine.

It seems the leaves now celebrate,
for autumn they no longer wait.

The wind initiates a dance
of diverse hues that all entrance.

The bronze ones dance with partners red,
with yellow, brown ones overhead.

Some leave their partners, float away,
while some upon the ground will play.

A wondrous time to cast your eyes
on autumn's colors, what a prize.

Section 5

Nature's Flowers

A Floral Kiss

My royal purple iris bloomed
    once more when springtime came.
This year they seemed indeed well groomed,
    as if placed in a frame.

The background of my dogwood tree
    with its fresh blooms in pink
created quite a color spree;
    so much more than you think.

The yellow buttercups below,
    wisteria up above,
azaleas, lilies in a row,
    the iris kiss with love.

Earth's Wonders

A daisy, rose, azalea,
are blooming in Australia,
when leaves fall in America.

Geography I like so much,
I've read of climates, temps, and such,
so much I see but cannot touch.

From hemisphere to hemisphere
the seasons own the atmosphere
today and even year to year.

The wonder of rain forests' clime,
or desert stillness, how sublime!
Their wonders transcend time on time.

A Morning Show

I wakened to azalea blooms
whose fragrance filled all of my rooms.
A perfumed magic filled the air
as if the blooms were everywhere.
One glance charmed everything in sight,
as did the prance of a bobwhite.
It seemed to stare at white and pink,
I wonder what bobwhites may think?
The blooms were pink, magenta, red,
the ones that I saw from my bed.
When I arose, what joy I knew;
from my own window, what a view!

Rose Petals

Where petals of red roses fall,
  a heavenly path of red
spreads like a giant colored shawl
  across a flower bed.

The petals lie there briefly till
  the wind puts them in flight;
like redbirds soaring at their will:
  rose petals, what a sight.

How high can soaring petals fly—
  to heights where winds can go?
A single rose cannot know why
  its petals blooms outgrow.

They spread the way for happy brides,
  adorn a loved one's grave.
Each petal of a rose provides
  a prized moment to save.

My First Buttercup

I looked across my bright green lawn
    and saw a blooming buttercup;
the first to open at the dawn
    of springtime; how it cheers me up.

The yellow cup with petals five
    now captures sunlight through the day
and nighttime's rain will make it thrive,
    perhaps to rest in a bouquet.

More nearby buds are poised to bloom
    with rising of the morning sun.
My flower bed I'll need not groom,
    for Mother Nature's work is done.

Gerber Daisies

I watched the Gerber daisies bloom
    outside my own front door.
Some yellow withered ones made room
    for two bright pink ones more.

The yellow ones lasted a week,
    their long stems regal, strong;
their petals slender, shiny, sleek
    in sunshine basked day long.

Some daisies' petals are bright white,
    and they have their appeal.
But colored Gerbers, what delight;
    their colors joy reveal.

I have not mentioned orange, red,
    such Gerbers I have too.
These colors grace my flower bed,
    but none of them is blue.

A White Gardenia

A white gardenia on a stem
    of green-leafed beauty bright,
without a doubt a nature gem,
    exquisite in sunlight.

Its crystal whiteness unsurpassed
    among my garden flowers,
the perfect color scheme contrast,
    now waiting springtime showers.

Gardenias

Gardenias by the garden wall
will every passerby enthrall.
Their fragrance and aroma sweet;
few flowers can with them compete.
Their gentle petals, soft and white,
reflect both moonbeams and sunlight.
You know them by their sight and smell.
Gardenias cast a unique spell.

Colorful Monet

Monet's stunning, lovely flowers,
    bright colored lily pads:
I love to observe for hours;
    colors he adds and adds.

Enchanting, wonderful Monet
    imbued with joy, delight.
The colors take your breath away
    by sun- or by moonlight.

You stop a moment, see his scenes,
    then linger while entranced;
you need not ask what each one means.
    Your spirit danced and danced.

The Daffodil

The day began with deep blue sky
in spite of rain clouds that passed by.
A bluebird on my window sill
stood right beside a daffodil
I planted in my window box
between some sleek, moss-covered rocks.
The bluebird stood and stared, it seemed,
as sunlight through my window streamed.
One moment it seemed that a trance
embraced the scene, then with a glance
the bluebird must have had its fill,
then left was just the daffodil.